Project Accounting

Steven M. Bragg

 AccountingTools®

ISBN 978-1-64221-159-7

For more information about AccountingTools® products, visit our Web site at www.accountingtools.com.

Table of Contents

About the Author

Steven Bragg, CPA, has been the chief financial officer or controller of four companies, as well as a consulting manager at Ernst & Young. He received a master's degree in finance from Bentley College, an MBA from Babson College, and a Bachelor's degree in Economics from the University of Maine. He has been a two-time president of the Colorado Mountain Club, and is an avid alpine skier, mountain biker, and certified master diver. Mr. Bragg resides in Centennial, Colorado. He has written more than 300 books and courses, including *New Controller Guidebook*, *GAAP Guidebook*, and *Payroll Management*.

Steven maintains the accountingtools.com web site, which contains continuing professional education courses, the Accounting Best Practices podcast, and thousands of articles on accounting subjects.

Buy Additional AccountingTools Courses

AccountingTools offers more than 1,500 hours of CPE courses, with concentrations in accounting, auditing, finance, taxation, and ethics. Related courses that you might like include:

- Construction Accounting
- Contract Management
- Financial Analysis
- Project Management

Go to accountingtools.com/cpe to view these additional courses.

AccountingTools®

Chapter 1
Overview of Project Accounting

Introduction

Projects are a necessary part of many business arrangements, and yet organizations frequently do not make any special provisions for the related accounting. Instead, business transactions related to projects are considered part of the general operations of a business, so their results are not broken out. A better approach is to develop project-specific billing, costing, and reporting systems. In this chapter, we begin the process of developing a system of accounting by discussing the nature of a project, the accounting decisions related to it, and the responsibilities of the project accountant.

The Project

A project is an activity that has the following characteristics:

- *The output is unique.* The activity is intended to produce a specific activity or product. This means that it does not produce an ongoing stream of goods or services, as would a production line or consulting practice.
- *There is a beginning and an end.* The activity has a clear start and end date. This means that it is not intended to continue in perpetuity, as would a functional area of a business, such as the production department.

EXAMPLE

The ancient firm of Monique Ponto creates small batches of watches and sells them to collectors. It usually takes four prototypes before a new watch model is ready for a limited production run. Each of the prototypes is considered a project, since the output is unique and there are clearly-defined start and stop dates associated with each prototype.

The production of the small batches of finalized watches cannot be considered projects, because their output is not unique (even though these production runs have clearly-defined start and stop dates).

There are many kinds of projects. Here are a few examples:

- A company sets up a team to see if a synthetic molecule can be converted into an anti-cancer treatment.
- A company conducts an investigation on behalf of the federal government into the technical difficulties involved in parachuting an astronaut to earth from orbit.

- A construction company contracts with a large local manufacturer to build a new production facility.
- A state government contracts with a software development company to create a new welfare payment management system for its citizens.

Whenever a project is created, it is necessary to track its performance to see if the desired outcome is acceptable, when balanced against the costs incurred. The purpose of this book is to describe the nature of the accounting for a project. This includes the following accounting tasks:

- Generating billings to customers, depending on the type of sales contract entered into with them.
- Recognizing revenue based on the dictates of Generally Accepted Accounting Principles (GAAP).
- Deciding which costs to charge to a project, how this information is to be recorded, and how it is to be presented in financial reports.
- How to monitor the costs incurred by a project, and what process to use to obtain additional revenue from customers.
- How to incorporate additional accounting concepts into a project, such as interest capitalization and asset impairment.
- Whether controls and measurements should be built into the system of accounting for a project, so that only necessary costs are incurred and there is a reasonable feedback loop to management.

Discussions of these topics are included in the following chapters.

The Project Accountant

Most of the personnel assigned to a project are specialists in the area at which the project is targeted. This means there will be a preponderance of scientists assigned to a research project, engineers to a product development effort, and trades personnel to the construction of an office building. However, all projects require a certain amount of administrative support, especially in the area of accounting.

A project accountant is usually assigned to any reasonably large project. This position is accountable for monitoring the progress of projects, investigating variances, and ensuring that project billings are issued to customers and payments collected. In certain cases where the accountant reports to the project manager, the accountant is also expected to approve expenses. The principal accountabilities of a project accountant are as follows:

Record Management

- Create project accounts in the accounting system
- Maintain project-related records, including contracts and change orders
- Authorize access to project accounts

- Authorize the transfer of expenses into and out of project-related accounts
- Close out project accounts upon project completion

Expense Oversight

- Review and approve supplier invoices related to a project
- Review and approve time sheets for work related to a project
- Review and approve overhead charges to be applied to a project
- Review account totals related to project assets and expenses
- Investigate project variances
- Confer with receivables staff regarding unpaid contract billings

Customer Billings

- Create or approve all project-related billings to customers
- Investigate all project expenses not billed to customers
- Approve the write off of any project-related billings that cannot be billed to or collected from customers

Management Reporting

- Report on project profitability to management
- Submit variance reports to management
- Report to management on any opportunities for additional billings
- Report to management regarding the remaining funding available for projects

Outside Party Reporting

- Respond to requests for more detail from customers
- Create and submit government reports and tax returns related to projects
- Compile information for internal and external auditors, as required

In some respects, the project accountant position is a derivation of the cost accountant position, since the bulk of the project activities relate to the examination and prediction of costs. However, the project accountant has a wider range of responsibilities, including billings, record management, reporting, and audit support. Consequently, the position can be considered a more advanced cost accounting position, and perhaps one that can be a stepping-stone to an assistant controller position.

Depending on the number and size of the projects currently being managed within a business, the project accounting staff might report directly to the controller, be managed by an intermediate level of supervision, or simply be considered part of the cost accounting staff's work load. In the following organization chart, we assume that there are several project accountants reporting to a project accounting manager, who in turn reports to the company controller.

Sample Organizational Structure Including Project Accountants

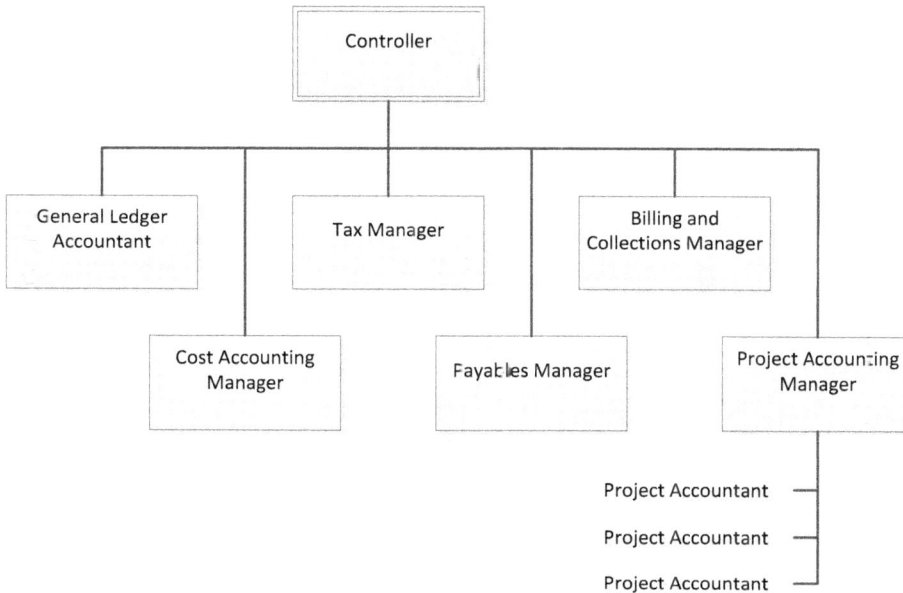

```
                          ┌─────────────┐
                          │ Controller  │
                          └──────┬──────┘
         ┌───────────────────────┼───────────────────────┐
┌────────────────┐      ┌────────────────┐      ┌──────────────────┐
│ General Ledger │      │  Tax Manager   │      │   Billing and    │
│   Accountant   │      │                │      │ Collections Mgr  │
└────────────────┘      └────────────────┘      └──────────────────┘
        ┌────────────────┐   ┌────────────────┐   ┌──────────────────┐
        │ Cost Accounting│   │ Fayables Manager│  │ Project Accounting│
        │    Manager     │   │                │   │     Manager      │
        └────────────────┘   └────────────────┘   └──────────────────┘
                                                            │
                                          Project Accountant ┤
                                          Project Accountant ┤
                                          Project Accountant ┤
```

Within a project, the project accountant acts as an advisor to, but not an employee of the project manager. This arrangement allows the accountant to forward information to the project manager regarding the revenue, cost and profit status of his or her project, without subjecting the accountant to any undue influence from the manager to present unusually rosy information about the status of the project.

Note: If the project accountant is not treated as an employee of the project manager, then responsibility for approving project expenses should shift to the manager. Otherwise, the accountant is approving expenses but has no responsibility for doing so.

Summary

A large part of this chapter has been concerned with the details of the project accountant position, because this is a necessary part of project accounting. If the company controller does not assign a specialist to monitor the financial aspects of projects, it is quite likely that any efforts in this area will be accorded secondary priority by the accounting staff. The result will likely be inaccurate or incomplete reporting of project results, missing or inaccurate customer billings, lost assets, and so forth. Consequently, accounting specialists are needed whenever an organization engages in projects that consume a significant proportion of company assets.

Chapter 2
Project Pricing, Billing and Revenue

Introduction

Some of the greatest complexity in project accounting relates to the recognition of revenue, especially when work is being conducted over a long period of time. There are a number of ways to determine the amount of revenue that should be recognized in each successive period of a contract, which can be impacted by changes in estimates and contract modifiers. In addition, the accountant must be aware of the pricing methodology used when the seller originally bid for a contract, since this impacts the nature of the billings sent to the customer. Finally, we note several issues relating to the structure of progress billings.

Project Pricing Methodologies

An activity worthy of separate project accounting is likely to have been obtained from a customer under a unique contractual arrangement. Under these contracts, the seller is either reimbursed for expenses incurred, or it commits to a fixed fee arrangement. In this section, we explore the cost plus pricing and fixed fee pricing concepts.

Cost Plus Pricing

Cost plus pricing is a cost-based method for setting the prices of goods and services under a contractual arrangement. The seller adds together the direct material cost, direct labor cost, and overhead costs for a project, and adds to it a markup percentage in order to derive the price to be billed. From the buyer's perspective, this can be an expensive pricing system, since costs may spiral well above initial expectations. However, it is an ideal system when there is a high degree of uncertainty regarding the design specifications of the final product.

A buyer is more likely to use this type of contract when its primary concerns are with the perceived capability and reliability of the seller, rather than with the ultimate cost of the contract. There is a reduced need to identify the precise deliverables as part of the initial contract. Instead, the seller may be asked to develop the project specifications in conjunction with the buyer once the contract has been awarded.

EXAMPLE

Cantilever Construction is bidding on a project that is expected to contain the following costs:

Direct material costs	$1,120,000
Direct labor costs	550,000
Allocated overhead	215,000
Total costs	$1,885,000

Under the terms of the proposed contract, the company is allowed to add a 10% markup to all of its products. To derive the estimated revenues to be gained from this contract, Cantilever adds together the stated costs to arrive at a total cost of $1,885,000, and then multiplies this amount by $(1 + 0.10)$ to arrive at the total contract price of $2,073,500.

The following are advantages of using the cost plus pricing method:

- *Simple.* It is quite easy to derive a bid price using this method, though it is necessary to define the overhead allocation method for costs that can be assigned to the project.
- *Assured contract profits.* Any seller is willing to accept this method for a contractual arrangement with a customer, since it is assured of having its costs reimbursed and of making a profit. There is no risk of loss on such a contract.
- *Justifiable.* In cases where the seller must persuade its customers of the need for a price increase, the seller can point to an increase in its costs as the reason for the price increase.

However, from the perspective of any customer that hires a seller under a cost plus pricing arrangement, the seller has no incentive to curtail its expenditures - on the contrary, it will likely include as many costs as possible in the contract so that it can be reimbursed. To combat this issue, a contractual arrangement may include cost-reduction incentives for the seller.

Fixed Fee Pricing

Fixed fee pricing occurs when the seller commits to being paid a fixed amount by the buyer. In this situation, the costs incurred by the seller have no impact on the price paid. This arrangement would appear to strongly favor the buyer, since there is no risk of paying more than the contract price. In fact, this arrangement is most common in a multi-party bidding scenario where a number of potential sellers are forced to bid against each other. However, there are two situations in which a fixed fee arrangement could favor the seller; they are:

- *Low-cost producer.* The seller may believe it can meet the buyer's requirements without incurring a significant cost overrun, and so feels comfortable in setting a price that will yield an unusually large profit. This can result in unethical behavior to minimize costs incurred to the point where the final product barely meets the quality standards of the buyer.

- *Contract additions.* The seller goes into the arrangement with the intent of creating additions to the contract whenever the buyer's specifications increase beyond the baseline established in the original contract. In this manner, the seller expects to earn a profit from change orders.

It is best from the perspectives of both the buyer and seller to create quite detailed specifications for a fixed fee contract, so there is little question about what is expected of the seller, and what constitutes an acceptable final product.

Fixed fee pricing tends to result in contract failure when there are significant uncertainties in a contract, such as the development of a new product that includes new technology. There can also be issues when there are numerous changes to the scope of the project, resulting in ongoing negotiations between the two parties to revise the contract. In these cases, it is better to adopt a cost plus pricing arrangement, where the seller will not be financially harmed if there is a legitimate cost overrun.

Contractual Modifiers

Both the cost plus and fixed fee contract types may have modifying clauses built into them, which can be used to modify the risks assumed by the two parties. Examples of these clauses are:

- *Guaranteed maximum.* The buyer seeks to keep the total cost of the contract from exceeding a certain amount. This clause can be a difficult one for the seller to accept, since it implies that the buyer will not impose too many scope changes once the initial contract has been signed. If a large number of scope changes are requested, the seller is likely to demand a renegotiation of the guaranteed maximum price.
- *Overrun cost sharing.* In a cost plus arrangement, the seller has no incentive to reduce its costs by targeting efficiencies. The buyer can demand an overrun cost sharing clause in order to incentivize the seller to manage its costs more effectively. Under this arrangement, a portion of each cost overrun must be absorbed by the seller, rather than being automatically passed through to the buyer.
- *Underrun profit sharing.* If costs are not as high as expected, the seller does not fare as well under a cost plus contract, since its profit will be reduced. The buyer can offer to mitigate this effect by splitting some portion of the cost savings with the seller.
- *Overrun penalty.* The buyer may want a threshold cost target, above which it sets a significant penalty that the seller will incur. This approach can also be targeted at a non-cost performance item, such as a penalty for every extra hour that a bridge construction project closes down a major highway.
- *Early delivery bonus.* If the buyer must obtain use of the final product as early as possible, it can offer an early delivery bonus. This bonus may be structured

to increase in size for an exceedingly early delivery, in order to provide a large incentive for the seller to use its best project planning staff.

The nature of the contractual modifiers used should be targeted at the precise nature of the contract. For example, do not provide an early delivery bonus if the buyer has no immediate need for the project deliverable.

Progress Billings

A longer-term project is likely to contain a contractual provision that allows the seller to issue progress billings to the buyer at regular intervals. These billings contain several features in addition to what is normally found on an invoice. The following supplemental information must typically be provided:

- *Project identifier*. The buyer may have assigned a project number or name to the seller, which must be included in every invoice to the buyer that relates to the project. The buyer needs this information in order to assign the billed amount to the correct account in its accounting system.
- *Task identifier*. Less frequently, the buyer may be tracking billed amounts by task within the overall project classification. If so, it may be necessary to break down the invoice so that separate billing line items cover each billed task.
- *Period covered*. State the specific period covered by the invoice. Some buyers want to see the exact date range, in which case the beginning and ending day, month, and year must be listed.

> **Tip:** The specifics used in a progress billing will vary by buyer, so it can make sense to include a billing summary sheet in the project billing folder for each project. Doing so makes it easier to produce consistent billings for each project.

When engaging in progress billings, it makes great sense to track all previously-issued invoices on an electronic spreadsheet. The intent behind doing so is to ensure that billings are only made in amounts that have already been funded as stated in the contract with the customer. Thus, any progress billing for an amount exceeding the pre-authorized amount will be immediately obvious before the invoice is issued. The following exhibit shows a sample layout for such a spreadsheet; the critical part of the exhibit is the cumulative billed amount column, which can be compared to the total authorized funding listed at the top of the same column.

Sample Progress Billing

Customer: Acme Development Project identifier: ACQ1040B		Authorized Funding:	$120,000
Billing Month	Invoice Number	Invoice Amount	Cumulative Amount
January 20X3	5301	$18,720	$18,720
February 20X3	5428	23,010	41,730
March 20X3	5611	28,650	70,380
April 20X3	5773	27,440	97,820

In the sample spreadsheet, the person tasked with project billings will need to closely monitor the work done on the project during the month of May, since it appears that the normal monthly billing rate will slightly exceed the authorized funding sometime towards the end of the month.

Project Revenue Recognition

When revenue is associated with a project, it is likely that the seller will be in a position to recognize revenue over multiple reporting periods. If so, the seller recognizes revenue through the application of a progress completion method. The goal of this method is to determine the progress of the seller in achieving complete satisfaction of its performance obligation under the terms of the project contract. According to the mandates of GAAP, this method is to be consistently applied over time, and shall be re-measured at the end of each reporting period.

Both output methods and input methods are considered acceptable for determining progress completion. The method chosen should incorporate due consideration of the nature of the goods or services being provided to the customer. The following subsections address the use of output and input methods.

Output Methods

An output method recognizes revenue based on a comparison of the value to the customer of goods and services transferred to date to the remaining goods and services not yet transferred. There are numerous ways to measure output, including:

- Surveys of performance to date
- Milestones reached
- The passage of time
- The number of units delivered
- The number of units produced

Another output method that may be acceptable is the amount of consideration that the seller has the right to invoice, such as billable hours. This approach works when the seller has a right to invoice an amount that matches the amount of performance completed to date.

The number of units delivered or produced may not be an appropriate output method in situations where there is a large amount of work-in-process, since the value associated with unfinished goods may be so substantial that revenue could be materially under-reported.

The method picked should closely adhere to the concept of matching the seller's progress toward satisfying the performance obligation. It is not always possible to use an output method, since the cost of collecting the necessary information can be prohibitive, or progress may not be directly observable.

Input Methods

An input method derives the amount of revenue to be recognized based on the to-date effort required by the seller to satisfy a performance obligation relative to the total estimated amount of effort required. Examples of possible inputs are costs incurred, labor hours expended, and machine hours used. If there are situations where the effort expended does not directly relate to the transfer of goods or services to a customer, do not use that input. The following are situations where the input used could lead to incorrect revenue recognition:

- The costs incurred are higher than expected, due to seller inefficiencies. For example, the seller may have wasted a higher-than-expected amount of raw materials in the performance of its obligations under a contract.
- The costs incurred are not in proportion to the progress of the seller toward satisfying the performance obligation. For example, the seller might purchase a large amount of materials at the inception of a project, which comprise a significant part of the total price.

> **Tip:** If the effort expended to satisfy performance obligations occur evenly through the performance period, consider recognizing revenue on the straight-line basis through the performance period.

EXAMPLE

Eskimo Construction is hired to build a weather observatory in Barrow, Alaska, which is estimated to be a six-month project. Utilities are a major concern, especially since the facility is too far away from town for a power line to be run out to it. Accordingly, a large part of the construction cost is a diesel-powered turbine generator. The total cost that Eskimo intends to incur for the project is:

Turbine cost	$1,250,000
All other costs	2,750,000
Total costs	$4,000,000

The turbine is to be delivered and paid for at the beginning of the construction project, but will not be incorporated into the facility until late summer, when the building is scheduled to be nearly complete.

Eskimo intends to use an input method to derive the amount of revenue, using costs incurred. However, this approach runs afoul of the turbine cost, since the immediate expenditure for the turbine gives the appearance of the project being 31.25% complete before work has even begun. Accordingly, Eskimo excludes the cost of the turbine from its input method calculations, only using the other costs as the basis for deriving revenue.

The situation described in the preceding example is quite common, since materials are typically procured at the inception of a project, rather than being purchased in equal quantities over the duration of the project. Consequently, the accountant should be particularly mindful of this issue and incorporate it into any revenue recognition calculations based on an input method.

A method based on output is preferred, since it most faithfully depicts the performance of the seller under the terms of a contract. However, an input-based method is certainly allowable if using it would be less costly for the seller, while still providing a reasonable proxy for the ongoing measurement of progress.

Change in Estimate

Whichever method is used, be sure to update it over time to reflect changes in the seller's performance to date. If there is a change in the measurement of progress, treat the change as a change in accounting estimate.

A change in accounting estimate occurs when there is an adjustment to the carrying amount of an asset or liability, or the subsequent accounting for it. Changes in accounting estimate occur relatively frequently, and so would require a significant effort to make an ongoing series of retroactive changes to prior financial statements. Instead, GAAP only requires that changes in accounting estimate be accounted for in the period of change and thereafter. Thus, no retrospective change is required or allowed.

Progress Measurement

It is only possible to recognize the revenue associated with progress completion if it is possible for the seller to measure the seller's progress. If the seller lacks reliable progress information, it will not be possible to recognize the revenue associated with a project over time. There may be cases where the measurement of progress completion is more difficult during the early stages of a project. If so, it is allowable for the seller to instead recognize just enough revenue to recover its costs in satisfying its performance obligations, thereby deferring the recognition of other revenue until such time as the measurement system yields more accurate results.

Percentage of Completion Method

A number of progress completion methods were described in the preceding section. In project accounting, the most common calculation technique used to apply the preceding alternatives is the percentage of completion method. This method involves, as the name implies, the ongoing recognition of revenue and income related to longer-term projects. By doing so, the seller can recognize some gain or loss related to a project in every accounting period in which the project continues to be active. The method works best when it is reasonably possible to estimate the stages of project completion on an ongoing basis, or at least to estimate the remaining costs to complete a project.

Conversely, this method should not be used when there are significant uncertainties about the percentage of completion or the remaining costs to be incurred (see the following Completed Contract Method section for an alternative approach). The estimating abilities of the seller should be considered sufficient to use the percentage of completion method if it can estimate the minimum total revenue and maximum total cost with sufficient confidence to justify a contract bid.

The ability to create dependable contract estimates may be impaired when there are conditions present that are not normally encountered in the estimating process. Examples of these conditions are when a contract does not appear to be enforceable, there is litigation, or when related properties may be condemned or expropriated. In these situations, use the completed contract method instead.

In essence, the percentage of completion method allows one to recognize as income that percentage of total income that matches the percentage of completion of a project. The percentage of completion may be measured in any of the following ways:

- *Cost-to-cost method.* This is a comparison of the contract cost incurred to date to the total expected contract cost. The cost of items already purchased for a contract but which have not yet been installed should not be included in the determination of the percentage of completion of a project, unless they were specifically produced for the contract. Also, allocate the cost of equipment over the contract period, rather than up-front, unless title to the equipment is being transferred to the customer.
- *Efforts-expended method.* This is the proportion of effort expended to date in comparison to the total effort expected to be expended for the contract. For example, the percentage of completion might be based on direct labor hours, or machine hours, or material quantities.
- *Units-of-delivery method.* This is the percentage of units delivered to the buyer to the total number of units to be delivered under the terms of a contract. It should only be used when the contractor produces a number of units to the specifications of a buyer. The recognition is based on:
  - For revenue, the contract price of units delivered
  - For expenses, the costs reasonably allocable to the units delivered

The steps needed for the percentage of completion method are as follows:

1. Subtract total estimated contract costs from total estimated contract revenues to arrive at the total estimated gross margin.
2. Measure the extent of progress toward completion, using one of the methods described above.
3. Multiply total estimated contract revenue by the estimated completion percentage to arrive at the total amount of revenue that can be recognized.
4. Subtract the contract revenue recognized to date through the preceding period from the total amount of revenue that can be recognized. Recognize the result in the current accounting period.
5. Calculate the cost of earned revenue in the same manner. This means multiplying the same percentage of completion by the total estimated contract cost, and subtracting the amount of cost already recognized to arrive at the cost of earned revenue to be recognized in the current accounting period.

This method is subject to fraudulent activity, usually to over-estimate the amount of revenue and profit that should be recognized. Detailed documentation of project milestones and completion status can mitigate the possibility of fraud, but cannot eliminate it.

EXAMPLE

Logger Construction Company is building a maintenance facility on a military base. Logger has thus far accumulated $4,000,000 of costs related to the project, and billed the customer $4,500,000. The estimated gross margin on the project is 20%. Therefore, the total of expenses and estimated gross profit for the project is:

$$\$4,000,000 \text{ Expenses} \div (1 - 0.20 \text{ Gross margin}) = \$5,000,000$$

Since this figure is higher than the to-date billings of $4,500,000, Logger can recognize additional revenue of $500,000, using the following journal entry:

	Debit	Credit
Unbilled contract receivables	500,000	
Contract revenue earned		500,000

Logger should also recognize a proportional amount of expense to offset the amount of revenue recognized, for which the calculation is:

$$\$500,000 \text{ Additional contract revenue} \times (1 - 0.20 \text{ Gross margin}) = \$400,000$$

13

Completed Contract Method

The completed contract method, as the name implies, is used to recognize all of the revenue and profit associated with a project only after the project has been completed. This method yields the same results as the percentage of completion method, but only after a project has been completed. Prior to completion, this method does not yield any useful information for the reader of a company's financial statements. However, the delay in income recognition allows a business to defer the recognition of related income taxes.

Also, since revenue and expense recognition only occurs at the end of a project, the timing of revenue recognition can be both delayed and highly irregular. Given these issues, the method should only be used under the following circumstances:

- When it is not possible to derive dependable estimates about the percentage of completion of a project; or
- When there are inherent hazards that may interfere with completion of a project; or
- When contracts are of such a short-term nature that the results reported under the completed contract method and the percentage of completion method would not vary materially.

If a contract is being accounted for under this method, record billings issued and costs incurred on the balance sheet during all periods prior to the completion of the contract, and then shift the entire amount of these billings and costs to the income statement upon completion of the underlying contract. A contract is assumed to be complete when the remaining costs and risks are insignificant.

If there is an expectation of a loss on a contract, record it at once even under the completed contract method; do not wait until the end of the project to do so.

EXAMPLE

Logger Construction Company is building housing for a disaster relief agency, and is doing so at great speed, so that displaced citizens can move in as soon as possible. Logger's management expects that the entire facility will be complete in just two months. Given the short duration of the project, Logger elects to use the completed contract method. Accordingly, Logger compiles $650,000 of costs on its balance sheet over the period of the project, and then bills the customer for the entire $700,000 fee associated with the project, recognizes the $650,000 of expenses, and recognizes a $50,000 profit.

Contract Modifications

A contract modification occurs when there is a scope or price change to the contract, and the change is approved by both signatories to the contract. Other terms may be used for a contract modification, such as a change order. It is possible that a contract modification exists, despite the presence of a dispute between the parties concerning scope or price. All of the relevant facts and circumstances must be considered when determining whether there is an enforceable contract modification that can impact revenue recognition.

If a change in contract scope has already been approved, but the corresponding change in price to reflect the scope change is still under discussion, the seller must estimate the change in price.

Treatment as Separate Contract

There are circumstances under which a contract modification might be accounted for as a separate contract. For this to be the case, the following two conditions must both be present:

- *Distinct change.* The scope has increased, to encompass new goods or services that are distinct from those offered in the original contract.
- *Price change.* The price has increased enough to encompass the standalone prices of the additional goods and services, adjusted for the circumstances related to that specific contract.

When these circumstances are met, there is an economic difference between a modified contract for the additional goods or services and a situation where an entirely new contract has been created.

EXAMPLE

Blitz Communications is buying one million experimental custom-designed cell phone batteries from Creekside Industrial, which is being accounted for by Creekside as a separate, unique project. The parties decide to alter the contract to add the purchase of 200,000 battery chargers for a price increase of $2.8 million. The associated price increase includes a 30% discount, which Creekside was already offering to Blitz under the terms of the original contract. This contract change reflects a distinct change that adds new goods to the contract, and includes an associated price change that has been adjusted for the discount terms of the contract. This contract modification can be accounted for as a separate contract, though the cost will be tracked within the same project.

Treatment as Continuing Contract

It may not be possible to treat a contract modification as a separate contract. If so, there are likely to be goods or services not yet transferred to the customer as of the modification date. The seller can account for these residual deliveries using one of the following methods:

- *Remainder is distinct.* If the remaining goods or services to be delivered are distinct from those already delivered under the contract, account for the modification as a cancellation of the old contract and creation of a new one. In this case, the consideration that should be allocated to the remaining performance obligations is the sum total of:

- o The original consideration promised by the customer but not yet received; and
- o The new consideration associated with the modification.

EXAMPLE

Nova Corporation contracts with the Deep Field Scanning Authority to construct two three-meter telescopes. The terms of the contract included a provision that could increase the allowable price charged by $250,000, with this price being apportioned equally between the two telescopes. One month into the contract period, Deep Field completely alters the configuration of the second telescope, from a reflector to a catadioptric model. The change is so significant that this telescope can now be considered a separate contract that will be tracked as a separate project. However, since the variable price was already apportioned at the inception of the original contract, the $125,000 allocated to each telescope will continue. This is because the variable consideration was promised prior to the contract modification.

- • *Remainder is not distinct.* If the remaining goods or services to be delivered are not distinct from those already delivered under the contract, account for the modification as part of the existing contract. This results in an adjustment to the recognized amount of revenue (up or down) as of the modification date. Thus, the adjustment involves calculating a change in the amount of revenue recognized on a cumulative catch-up basis.

EXAMPLE

Domicilio Corporation enters into a contract to construct the world headquarters building of the International Mushroom Farmers' Cooperative. Mushroom requires its architects to be true to the name of the organization, with the result being a design for a squat, dark building with no windows, high humidity, and a unique waste recycling system. Domicilio has not encountered such a design before, and so incorporates a cautious stance into its assumptions regarding the contract terms.

The contract terms state that Domicilio will be paid a total of $12,000,000, broken into a number of milestone payments. There is also a $100,000 on-time completion bonus. At the inception of the contract, Domicilio expects the following financial results:

Transaction price	$12,000,000
Expected costs	9,000,000
Expected profit (25%)	$3,000,000

The project manager anticipates trouble with several parts of the construction project, and advises strongly against including any part of the completion bonus in the transaction price.

At the end of seven months, the project manager is surprised to find that Domicilio is on target to complete the work on time. Also, the company has completed 65% of its performance obligation, based on the $5,850,000 of costs incurred to date relative to the total amount of expected costs. Through this point, the company has recognized the following revenues and costs:

Revenue	$7,800,000
Costs	5,850,000
Gross profit	$1,950,000

The project manager is still uncomfortable with recognizing any part of the completion bonus.

With one month to go on the project, the project manager finally allows that Domicilio will likely complete the project one week early, though he has completely lost all interest in eating mushrooms. At this point, the company has completed 92.5% of its performance obligation (based on costs incurred), so the project accountant recognizes an additional $92,500 for that portion of the $100,000 on-time completion bonus that has already been earned.

- *Mix of elements.* If the remaining goods or services to be delivered are comprised of a mix of distinct and not-distinct elements, separately identify the different elements and account for them as per the dictates of the preceding two methods.

Entitlement to Payment

At all points over the duration of a contract, the seller should have the right to payment for the performance completed to date, if the customer were to cancel the contract for reasons other than the seller's failure to perform. The amount of this payment should approximate the selling price of the goods or services transferred to the customer to date; this means that costs are recovered, plus a reasonable profit margin. This reasonable profit margin should be one of the following:

- A reasonable proportion of the expected profit margin, based on the extent of the total performance completed prior to contract termination; or
- A reasonable return on the cost of capital that the seller has experienced on its cost of capital for similar contracts, if the margin on this particular contract is higher than the return the seller typically generates from this type of contract.

An entitlement to payment depends on contractual factors, such as only being paid when certain milestones are reached or when the customer is completely satisfied with a deliverable. There may not be an entitlement to payment if one of these contractual factors is present. Further, there may be legal precedents or legislation that may interfere with or bolster an entitlement to payment. For example:

- There may be a legal precedent that gives the seller the right to payment for all performance to date, even though this right is not clarified within the contract terms.

17

- Legal precedent may reveal that other sellers having similar rights to payment in their contracts have not succeeded in obtaining payment.
- The seller may not have attempted to enforce its right to payment in the past, which may have rendered its rights legally unenforceable.

Conversely, the terms of a contract may not legally allow a customer to terminate a contract. If so, and the customer still attempts to terminate the contract, the seller may be entitled to continue to provide goods or services to the customer, and require the customer to pay the amounts stated in the contract. In this type of situation, the seller has an enforceable right to payment.

An enforceable right to payment may not match the payment schedule stated in a contract. The payment schedule does not necessarily sync with the seller's right to payment for performance. For example, the customer could have insisted upon delayed payment dates in the payment schedule in order to more closely match its ability to make payments to the seller.

EXAMPLE

A customer of Hodgson Industrial Design pays a $50,000 nonrefundable upfront payment to Hodgson at the inception of a contract to overhaul the design of the customer's main product. The customer does not like Hodgson's initial set of design prototypes, and cancels the contract. On the cancellation date, Hodgson's billable hours on the project sum to $65,000. Hodgson has an enforceable right to retain the $50,000 it has already been paid. The right to be paid for the remaining $15,000 depends on the contract terms and legal precedents.

Measurement of Progress Completion

A seller might be tempted to create an elaborate new system to measure its progress toward completing various performance obligations under a contract. However, any new measurement system imposes an administrative cost, especially if it is in addition to existing measurement systems. Consequently, it can be better to continue using an existing progress measurement system, unless its results are significantly altering revenue recognition from what it should be.

If management is contemplating a change to a new measurement system, it would be both useful and cost-effective to first use the new system on a pilot basis to determine its impact on revenue recognition. The results could be shared with the auditors to see if they agree with the new system, and then incorporate any necessary revisions into the system before rolling it out throughout the business. Otherwise, management may be startled to find that its recognized revenue levels are unusually high, low, or variable in relation to the previous situation.

Summary

As noted in this chapter, there are a number of GAAP-mandated revenue recognition rules that impact project accounting. However, as noted in the Entitlement to Payment section, the specific clauses in a customer contract regarding the right to payment can alter the amount of revenue recognized. For example, if a customer can refuse to accept the final deliverable, and has a history of doing so, the circumstances may dictate that all revenue recognition is deferred until after customer acceptance has occurred. Consequently, a thorough reading of the terms of the contract associated with a project is needed in order to determine the most appropriate revenue recognition methodology. It is helpful to document the results of this analysis, in order to justify to the company's auditors the revenue recognition for each project.

Chapter 3
Project Costs

Introduction

When setting up the accounting for a project, a number of issues should be considered – which costs will be charged to the project, how these costs will be collected and organized into expense classifications, and how this information will be tracked in the accounting system. In this chapter, we address each concern, and also note how to treat any costs incurred to obtain a contract.

Project Costs

The key aspect of the project accountant's job is to report on the costs associated with a project. What is a cost? It is an expenditure required to engage in an activity or to acquire an asset. This is almost always measured in monetary terms, so that hours incurred and materials acquired are recorded in the amount paid for them. The concept of cost is critical from a project perspective, since most projects are intended to create value for an organization, and the cost of a project must be determined in order to calculate the net amount of value created. In this section, we address the nature of direct costs and overhead costs, and note whether they should be charged to a project.

Direct Costs

Direct costs are those costs that would not exist if a project did not exist. In general, these costs should be charged to a project.

An example of a direct cost is materials purchased specifically for work being performed within a project. The cost of personnel salaries and their associated payroll taxes and benefits are also considered to be direct costs, on the assumption that these people would not be employed by the company if the project did not exist. In reality, many employees would be held in reserve over the short term if there were no project-related employment for them. Alternatively, employees may split their time between multiple projects, in which case they are expected to charge their time to the projects on which they are employed.

Other direct costs involve the use of equipment. This may include the purchased or rental cost of tools or heavier equipment. If the company already owns certain fixed assets and is lending them to a project, it is reasonable to charge the project for their use, based on the market rate at which similar assets could be rented from a third party.

Some direct costs are only associated with projects, or at least are rarely found outside of them. Examples are:

- *Performance bond fee.* This is a bond for which a customer is the beneficiary, guaranteeing that the seller managing a project will perform the services specified in the underlying contract.
- *Software licenses.* A project may need to pay for additional software licenses for the software that will be used by the project team for the duration of a project.
- *Contractors.* Contractors with special skill sets may be needed for a project. If there were no project, the contractors would not be needed.

Overhead Costs

Overhead costs are those costs need to run a business, but for which there is no clear cause-and-effect relationship with a business activity, product, or service. Examples of overhead costs are marketing, accounting, and legal services. One of the main arguments in project accounting is the extent to which overhead costs should be included in a project. The argument against their inclusion is that these costs would still exist even in the absence of a project. Conversely, if a company is in the business of running large billable projects on behalf of its customers, there must be a way to pass these costs through to the customer, particularly when cost plus contracts are involved. Possible ways to handle overhead costs are as follows:

- *Cost plus contracts.* There is a negotiation between the seller and the customer in regard to which overhead costs will be allowed to be charged to a specific contract. The seller will push for the largest amount possible, since this cost will be reimbursed by the customer.
- *Fixed fee contracts.* Additional revenue to be gained from a customer under a fixed fee contract will only occur when there is a change order request, and such a request will only be triggered by a scope change – not by a change in the overhead cost. Consequently, there is little point in allocating overhead to a fixed fee project.
- *Internal projects.* The application of overhead to an internal project will not generate any revenue, as would be the case with a cost plus contract. Consequently, there is no point in allocating overhead to an internal project.

In short, overhead costs are not directly related to the activities conducted within projects, and so should only be charged to them when doing so will generate revenue. Otherwise, the application of overhead to a project merely serves to inflate its cost.

Capitalized Interest

If an organization must take on debt in order to pay for construction within a project, it is reasonable to capitalize the cost of the interest into the project. Interest capitalization can be useful when passing through costs to a customer under a cost plus contract, or when constructing an asset for internal use. The interest capitalization concept is discussed further in the Interest Capitalization chapter.

Costs to Obtain a Contract

An organization may incur certain costs to obtain a contract with a customer that supports a project. If so, it is allowable to record these costs as an asset, and amortize them over the life of the contract. The following conditions apply:

- The costs must be incremental; that is, they would not have been incurred if the organization had not obtained the contract.
- If the amortization period will be one year or some lesser period, it is allowable to simply charge these costs to expense as incurred.
- There is an expectation that the costs will be recovered.

An example of a contract-related cost that could be recorded as an asset and amortized is the sales commission associated with a sale, though as a practical expedient it is usually charged to expense as incurred.

EXAMPLE

A water engineering firm bids on a contract to investigate the level of silt accumulation in the Oswego Canal in New York, and wins the bid. The firm incurs the following costs as part of its bidding process:

Staff time to prepare proposal	$18,000
Printing fees	2,500
Travel costs	5,000
Commissions paid to sales staff	15,000
	$40,500

The firm must charge the staff time, printing fees, and travel costs to expense as incurred, since it would have incurred these expenses even if the bid had failed. Only the commissions paid to the sales staff can be considered a contract asset, since that cost should be recovered through its future billings for consulting services.

When contract-related costs have been recognized as assets, they should be amortized on a systematic basis that reflects the timing of the transfer of related goods and services to the customer. If there is a change in the anticipated timing of the transfer of goods and services to the customer, update the amortization to reflect this change. This is considered a change in accounting estimate.

Information Organization and Presentation

A central issue in project accounting is how to organize the cost information that is to be collected for each separate project. This is not a minor task, for it may be necessary to create an entirely new account code structure for each project, depending on the types of costs that will be incurred. For example, a research and development project might require a number of cost categories to reflect the use of subcontracted testing services, while a software development project might instead require cost categories targeted at different types of software development contractors.

> **Tip:** If the company engages in a number of similar types of projects, try to use the same account code structure for all of them, so that the coding of expenses by the accounts payable staff can be as consistent as possible.

The organization of information for a project centers on a separate, project-specific income statement that lays out major categories of expenses, as well as a small number of line items to reflect the nature of any revenue received. The layout of this income statement tends to be smaller than what is used for the income statement that shows the results of an entire company. A sample project income statement appears in the following exhibit.

Sample Project Income Statement

Creekside Industrial
Battery Development Project
Income Statement
For the month ended October 31, 20X3

Project revenue	$700,000
Materials consumed	$80,000
Internal labor	230,000
Payroll taxes	15,000
Employee benefits	45,000
Contracted testing services	180,000
Equipment rental	50,000
Travel and entertainment	62,000
Supplies consumed	29,000
Total expenses	$691,000
Profit	$9,000

The sample project income statement has several characteristics not found on a company-wide income statement. These differences are:

- *Subtotals*. There is no need to break out a separate cost of goods sold subtotal, since doing so would imply that a project is operational in nature and so would continue to produce a cost of goods sold and a gross margin for the foreseeable future.
- *Single revenue line item*. The revenue associated with a project tends to be quite simple, usually involving a single contract. A number of revenue line items would imply that a project is actually a separate, long-term business that should be accounted for as a subsidiary.
- *Taxes*. No provision is made for income taxes. Though this could be done, it introduces an additional level of complexity to the project accounting that is not necessary. Instead, taxes are dealt with at the level of the corporate income statement.
- *Ordering of line items*. There is no set order in which the expense line items should be presented. It could be in alphabetical order, or in declining order by the size of expenses incurred. The presentation in the exhibit roughly mimics a traditional income statement, where materials and labor are noted first, followed by administrative expenses.

There is usually no need to produce a balance sheet for a project, detailing the assets allocated to and obligations of the project. Doing so usually provides little additional information to the project manager, who is likely more concerned with the amount of project-to-date expenses incurred. If there are reasons for doing so, it may be acceptable to maintain an informal listing of assets and liabilities on a separate spreadsheet. Taking this informal approach reduces the amount of project accounting labor that would otherwise be needed to set up additional project-specific accounts and shift assets and liabilities into them.

Information Recordation

How is information to be recorded for a project? There are several possibilities, ranging from being tightly integrated into the existing accounting system to an informal approach that is entirely separate. In this section, we address the alternatives, along with the advantages and disadvantages of each one.

Separate Spreadsheet

The most informal type of recordation system applies when a business rarely engages in project accounting, and the amount of funds allocated to a project is relatively small. In this case, it can make sense to simply track project revenues and expenses on a separate spreadsheet, while storing all information within the normal account structure of the company's general ledger. In this situation, the project accountant is provided with a list of the employees whose pay should be assigned to the project, the names of the contractors also providing services for the project, and the contract number under which billings are sent to a customer (if the project is a billable one). This information is then used to track down revenues and expenses in the regular accounting system and copy them over into the spreadsheet. The key advantage of this approach is that no changes need to be made to the corporate accounting system. In addition, the accounts payable staff does not need to use any special coding to assign supplier invoices to a project. However, the following problems are associated with the use of spreadsheets:

- *Inaccuracy.* It is entirely possible, if not likely, that the project accountant will forget to transfer some revenue and expense transactions from the main accounting system to the spreadsheet.
- *Missing expenses.* Additional expenses may be incurred by a project that were not anticipated when the project accountant was given the initial list of employees and suppliers whose expenses were to be charged to the project.
- *Lack of control.* The information in a spreadsheet can be easily altered to yield results that do not reflect the actual outcome of a project.

Separate General Ledger / Subledger Accounts

A more formal system is to create a separate account for a project in the chart of accounts. By doing so, all expenses related to a project are assigned to the designated project at the point of recordation. If this approach threatens to overwhelm the general ledger with too many transactions, the recordation could instead take place in a subledger, for which only the monthly totals are carried forward to the general ledger. The advantage of this option is that the accounting for a project becomes part of the normal operations of the accounting department. This option works well when a project is so large that its expenses form a significant proportion of the total expenses of a business. However, this alternative suffers from the following issues:

- *General ledger clutter.* If there are a number of projects, assigning a separate account to each one can soon clutter up the general ledger. Also, these records are now a permanent part of the general ledger, and so will be archived and maintained for a number of years to come.
- *Missing coding.* It is entirely possible that the accounts payable staff will not recognize a supplier invoice as being associated with a specific project, and so will instead code the invoice to a default expense account. This issue can be mitigated by issuing a regularly-updated listing of projects and related suppliers to the payables staff.
- *Single account coding.* This coding methodology merely charges all expenses to a single project account, without regard to the nature of each expense. The result is a single, aggregated expense number that the project accountant must further refine into different expense categories, such as contractors, project supplies, and equipment rental.

Separate Accounting Module

Some accounting software packages include a separate module that is specifically designed for the tracking of revenues and expenses related to projects. The general process flow for these modules is that a user is given the option to record a revenue or expense against a specific project, and is then given a list of open projects from which to choose, and a list of acceptable project accounts to which a transaction can be charged. This approach is the most organized and error-free approach to information recordation. However, this module is usually only available for the more expensive accounting software packages, and so may not be an option. Other than cost, the only real issue with a separate accounting module is that accounting employees may still not realize that expenses are to be charged to a specific project, and so will need reminding, possibly through a regularly-updated memo.

Information Collection

When tracking costs for a project, a key issue to address is the level of detail that should be collected. This is of particular concern under a cost plus contract or a fixed fee arrangement where the company wants to apply for a change order; in both cases, there must be a sufficient level of evidence that a customer's audit team would agree with the company regarding the nature of an expense that is being billed to them.

The level of information collection is relatively easy for supplier invoices. It is usually acceptable to note the supplier's invoice number, expense amount, and expense classification in the project records. If a customer's auditor wants further information, the invoice number can be used to locate the original invoice, which can then be forwarded to the customer.

The situation is different when payroll records are involved. If a customer is monitoring the company's compensation expenses at the individual task level, then everyone involved with the project must record their time at the task level, rather than just recording their time against the general identification code for the entire project. This can represent a major additional use of staff time, especially if they are working on several tasks within one or more projects. Nonetheless, if customers insist on this level of detail, then the timekeeping system must provide task codes for each project.

> **Tip:** Closely monitor when tasks have been completed on a project, and immediately deactivate the related task codes in the timekeeping system, so that employees and contractors do not incorrectly charge their time to these tasks.

Summary

If a business has a large number of projects, it will be at risk of having a tangled cost collection system that applies different types of direct and overhead costs to each project, uses different reporting structures, and collects different levels of information for each project. To some extent, these issues are related to the cost reporting requirements of customers, and so cannot be standardized. However, an attempt should be made to initially apply a standard definition of costs to each project, along with a standard reporting structure and cost collection system. Doing so at least provides a baseline for a consistent costing system for each project, which in turn can improve the efficiency of the project accountant.

Chapter 4
Project Cost Management

Introduction

The management of project costs is closely tied to a system for tracking project progress. The project manager must understand the amount of costs incurred so far, as well as the best estimate of costs still to be incurred. Doing so requires the detailed accumulation of historical and estimated costs on an ongoing basis. In addition, the project accountant can work on refining the level of certainty regarding the types and amounts of costs that will be incurred, which reduces the need for allowances and contingencies, and also yields insights into the types of cost variances incurred. Finally, an ongoing change order management system is needed to ensure that the seller can recover its costs when a scope change is proposed. These issues are discussed in the following sections.

Progress Monitoring

At the start of a project, the estimated amount of costs to be incurred is likely to be significantly different from the amount actually incurred. The project accountant needs a tool to monitor the progress of the project as a whole, and especially its historical and projected costs. This progress monitoring system is so important that it cannot be a casual affair that is thrown together. Instead, a business that deals with projects on a regular basis should consider purchasing an off-the-shelf software package that contains the core functionality of a progress monitoring system, and apply it religiously to every project.

When using a progress monitoring system, the main consideration is which progress indicators to use. Simply accumulating the cost incurred is not sufficient, since it does not necessarily reflect the amount of progress toward achieving the goal of the project. In addition to cost accumulation, the system should also report on what has been delivered, while also giving some indication of the rate of resource consumption. For example, the system could track the following additional information:

- Hours spent to date on each task
- Hours estimated to complete each task
- Cost incurred to date on each task
- Cost estimated to still be incurred on each task

It may be possible to replace or supplement these generic indicators of progress with more specific operational activities. For example, for a construction project, the system might track cubic yards of concrete poured or square yards of tile installed. Or, for a programming project, the system might track the number of reports configured or the number of lines of software code written.

Though a progress monitoring system is important, updating it should not interfere with the ongoing operations of a project team. Instead, minimize its time requirements by limiting the amount of information that is tracked and the frequency with which updates are required.

The outputs of the system should be reports that note those tasks completed, tasks still remaining, costs incurred, and estimated costs still to be incurred. These reports are used to draw management attention to those specific facets of a project that are incurring higher costs than expected, so that action can be taken to keep the cost variances from expanding further. This may result in changes in the scope of a project, changes in the due date, or alterations in the amount billed to the customer (if this is a billable situation).

Cost Variance Reporting

Part of the ongoing reporting for a project is to state the cost variances associated with it. However, dropping a lump sum cost variance into a report does little to inform managers about the reasons for the variance. Instead, the accountant should delve deeper into the reasons for a variance, which allows for categorization of the variance. For example, the following classifications could be used:

- *Budgeting errors*. A variance could have occurred because the original project plan did not call for a sufficiently large expense budget.
- *Implementation problems*. The initial budget might be correct, but the implementation has not gone well, perhaps due to having the wrong staff, low-quality materials, or flaws in the work product.
- *Scope change*. There may be a scope change for which there is not a sufficiently large offsetting change order, resulting in a net variance.
- *Time compression*. The customer may require that the timeline of the project be compressed. If so, this can trigger physical congestion as more workers are assigned to the project for a shorter period of time, which causes slowdowns. Overtime costs are also likely to increase. Conversely, a delay in completion can also increase costs, due to reduced team interaction and the deterioration of the team's memory regarding the optimal way to complete tasks.
- *Unexpected events*. There may be a natural disaster or an unforeseen event that impacts the ability of the team to complete the project.

Change Order Management

When a project involves billing a customer under a fixed fee arrangement, there is a strong likelihood that the scope of the project will change over time. If so, it will be necessary for the seller and its customer to mutually agree upon a change order that specifies the extent of the scope change, as well as the related alteration in the amount that the seller is now allowed to bill to the customer.

29

A change order management process involves a committee that is comprised of the project manager, a customer representative, and the project accountant. The manager and customer representative must approve each change order, while the accountant processes the paperwork for the change order and bills it to the customer. Various technical personnel from the project team will be brought in to discuss the financial and timing impact of proposed changes to the existing project scope. The committee is also responsible for maintaining the most current listing of project requirements, and for monitoring the project's actual status in comparison to these requirements.

Change requests should be documented on a standardized form, which ensures that the same set of information is provided to the committee whenever a change is proposed. The form should include space for the following information:

- *Change request number.* Needed to uniquely identify each request made. This is useful for ensuring that no requests are lost.
- *Name of the individual requesting the change.* Needed in order to report back the committee's decision, as well as to contact for more information. This field can include contact information for the requester.
- *Date of the request.* Needed to establish the amount of time that has elapsed before a request is dealt with.
- *Description of the change.* Summarizes the requested change, possibly including an estimate of the impact on project cost, scope, or time of completion.

When the committee receives a change request, it should enter the request into a change order log, so that no forms are inadvertently lost. The log should also state when the committee dealt with each request, and the outcome of that analysis. Once a change order is approved by the committee, the project accountant should enter it into a separate log that is used for billing purposes, to ensure that each change order is billed to the customer when the related work is completed.

Allowance Management

An allowance is a lump-sum estimate that is included in the project budget in place of more precise estimates. An allowance is used when a more specific initial determination of cost cannot be made. For example, a common project cost is travel and entertainment expense. At the start of a lengthy project, it may not be possible to determine when or how frequently employees will need to travel to a customer's site for meetings. In this situation, an allowance is created that is assumed to be in the general vicinity of the amount that will eventually be expended.

The excessive use of allowances makes it difficult to determine when the amount of costs incurred to date is reasonable or not. This level of uncertainty can be mitigated by minimizing the use of allowances. Ideally, they should be limited to a small proportion of the total project expense. Also, as a project progresses, attempt to reduce the amount of allowances in the project budget by increasing the certainty of certain expenditures, and shifting the required funds out of the allowances figure and into the designated budget line items. The result should be a project that starts with a number of allowances in different areas of the project budget, but which experiences a gradual re-apportionment of allowance funds to more concrete line items as the project progresses.

Contingency Management

A contingency is a buffer of additional funds added to a project budget, which is used to compensate for possible inaccuracies in the budget. The contingency buffer is used to deal with expenditures that were not expected at the start of a project. The contingency can be quite large when a project involves significant technical uncertainty, or if the seller does not have much experience in the area. As a project progresses, the project accountant should report to management on the remaining size of the contingency and the additional expenses for which the contingency was used.

It is important to only use the contingency to cover expenses that are the responsibility of the company. In a fixed fee arrangement, the contingency is to be avoided when a customer wants to increase the scope of the project. In this situation, the project manager should instead negotiate with the customer to create a change order that increases the amount billed to the customer. The worst situation is to avoid a change order by using the contingency fund to absorb a customer's scope requests; doing so reduces or eliminates the seller's profit.

Budget Accuracy

When the parameters for an initial project budget are excessively vague, the project team should be aware of the limitations of its budget. In this situation, it is best to continually revise the budget as better information becomes available. These revisions may not necessarily alter the total expected expenditure for a project, but may very well alter the allocation of funding between different line items in the budget.

The Sunk Cost Consideration

When engaging in project cost analysis where there is no customer reimbursement of costs, a series of unfavorable cost variances may spark comments from the project team that a further investment is needed to complete the project and recoup the earlier investment. Investing more funds in this situation may not be a good idea, since the earlier investment (known as a sunk cost) cannot be recovered. Instead, management must be more concerned with the tradeoff between the funds yet to be spent and the eventual return to be gained from the project. If the projected return has fallen so low that there is uncertainty about recouping even the remaining amount of funding not yet committed, then the best decision may be to cancel the project entirely.

Summary

It is relatively easy for a project accountant to report on the costs incurred thus far. A much more challenging task is to estimate the amount of costs yet to be incurred, since this relates to changes in the scope of a project, changes in the completion date, project team inefficiencies, technical problems, and so forth. A reasonable case can be made that the typical project accountant does not have the training to unilaterally make this estimate. Instead, it is necessary to coordinate closely with the project manager in devising cost estimates, since the project manager is in the best position to estimate the additional effort required, and whether any bottlenecks in the process could represent a serious delay.

The project accountant and project manager should also coordinate how changes in project costs are to be communicated to project stakeholders, since significant changes may trigger negative reactions.

Chapter 5
Interest Capitalization

Introduction

A project may be created in order to separately track the creation of a large asset. If the asset is to be used internally and the company incurred debt to build the asset, it should capitalize the interest expense associated with the asset. Also, depending on the contract terms, if the company is constructing an asset for a customer, it may be allowed to include the cost of interest expense in the billable amount of the project. In either case, the accountant should know the GAAP rules for capitalizing interest, which are discussed in this chapter.

Overview of Capitalized Interest

Interest is a cost of doing business, and if a company incurs an interest cost that is directly related to an asset, it is reasonable to capitalize this cost, since it provides a truer picture of the total investment in the asset. Since a business would not otherwise have incurred the interest if it had not acquired the asset, the interest is essentially a direct cost of owning the asset.

Conversely, if a business does not capitalize this interest cost and instead charges it to expense, the entity would be unreasonably reducing the amount of reported earnings during the period when the company incurred the expense, and increasing earnings during later periods, when it would otherwise have been charging the capitalized interest to expense through depreciation.

> **Tip:** If the amount of interest that may be applied to an asset is minor, try to avoid capitalizing it. Otherwise, you will spend extra time documenting the capitalization, and the auditors will spend time investigating it – which may translate into higher audit fees.

The value of the information provided by capitalizing interest may not be worth the effort of the incremental accounting cost associated with it. Here are some issues to consider when deciding whether to capitalize interest:

- How many assets would be subject to interest capitalization?
- How easy is it to separately identify those assets that would be subject to interest capitalization?
- How significant would be the effect of interest capitalization on the company's reported resources and earnings?

Thus, only capitalize interest when the informational benefit derived from doing so exceeds the cost of accounting for it. The positive impact of doing so is greatest for construction projects, where:

- Costs are separately compiled
- Construction covers a long period of time
- Expenditures are large
- Interest costs are significant

When to Capitalize Interest

Capitalize interest that is related to the following types of fixed assets:

- Assets that are constructed for the company's own use. This includes assets built for the company by suppliers, where the company makes progress payments or deposits.
- Assets that are constructed for sale or lease, and which are constructed as discrete projects.

EXAMPLE

Milford Sound builds a new corporate headquarters. The company hires a contractor to perform the work, and makes regular progress payments to the contractor. Milford should capitalize the interest expense related to this project.

Milford Sound creates a subsidiary, Milford Public Sound, which builds custom-designed outdoor sound staging for concerts and theatre activities. These projects require many months to complete, and are accounted for as discrete projects. Milford should capitalize the interest cost related to each of these projects.

If a company is undertaking activities to develop land for a specific use, capitalize interest related to the associated expenditures for as long as the development activities are in progress.

Do not capitalize interest that is related to the following types of fixed assets:

- Assets that are already in use or ready for their intended use
- Assets not being used, and which are not being prepared for use
- Assets not included in the company's balance sheet
- Inventories that are routinely manufactured

The Interest Capitalization Period

Capitalize interest over the period when there are ongoing activities to prepare a fixed asset for its intended use, but only if expenditures are actually being made during that time, and interest costs are being incurred.

EXAMPLE

Milford Public Sound is constructing an in-house sound stage in which to test its products. It spent the first two months designing the stage, and then paid a contractor $30,000 per month for the next four months to build the stage. Milford incurred interest costs during the entire time period.

Since Milford was not making any expenditures related to the stage during the first two months, it cannot capitalize any interest cost for those two months. However, since it was making expenditures during the next four months, it can capitalize interest cost for those months.

If a company stops essentially all construction on a project, stop capitalizing interest during that period. However, continue to capitalize interest under any of the following circumstances:

- Brief construction interruptions
- Interruptions imposed by an outside entity
- Delays that are an inherent part of the asset acquisition process

EXAMPLE

Milford Public Sound is constructing a concert arena that it plans to lease to a local municipality upon completion. Midway through the project, the municipality orders a halt to all construction, when construction reveals that the arena is being built on an Indian burial ground. Two months later, after the burial site has been relocated, the municipality allows construction to begin again.

Since this interruption was imposed by an outside entity, Milford can capitalize interest during the two-month stoppage period.

A company should terminate interest capitalization as soon as an asset is substantially complete and ready for its intended use. Here are several scenarios showing when to terminate interest capitalization:

- *Unit-level completion.* Parts of a project may be completed and usable before the entire project is complete. Stop capitalizing interest on each of these parts as soon as they are substantially complete and ready for use.
- *Entire-unit completion.* All aspects of an asset may need to be completed before any part of it can be used. Continue capitalizing interest on such assets until the entire project is substantially complete and ready for use.
- *Dependent completion.* An asset may not be usable until a separate project has also been completed. Continue capitalizing interest on such assets until not only the specific asset, but also the separate project is substantially complete and ready for use.

EXAMPLE

Milford Public Sound is building three arenas, all under different circumstances. They are:

1. *Arena A.* This is an entertainment complex, including a stage area, movie theatre, and restaurants. Milford should stop capitalizing interest on each component of the project as soon as it is substantially complete and ready for use, since each part of the complex can operate without the other parts being complete.

2. *Arena B.* This is a single outdoor stage with integrated multi-level parking garage. Even though the garage is completed first, Milford should continue to capitalize interest for it, since the garage is only intended to service patrons of the arena, and so will not be operational until the arena is complete.

3. *Arena C.* This an entertainment complex for which Milford is also constructing a highway off-ramp and road that leads to the complex. Since the complex is unusable until patrons can reach the complex, Milford should continue to capitalize interest expenses until the off-ramp and road are complete.

Do not continue to capitalize interest when completion is being deliberately delayed, since the cost of interest then changes from an asset acquisition cost to an asset holding cost.

EXAMPLE

The CEO of Milford Sound wants to report increased net income for the upcoming quarter, so he orders the delay of construction on an arena facility that would otherwise have been completed, so that the interest cost related to the project will be capitalized. He is in error, since this is now treated as a holding cost – the related interest expense should be recognized in the period incurred, rather than capitalized.

The Capitalization Rate

The amount of interest cost to capitalize for a fixed asset is that amount of interest that would have been avoided if the company had not acquired the asset. To calculate the amount of interest cost to capitalize, multiply the capitalization rate by the average amount of expenditures that accumulate during the construction period.

The basis for the capitalization rate is the interest rates that are applicable to the company's borrowings that are outstanding during the construction period. If a specific borrowing is incurred in order to construct a specific asset, use the interest rate on that borrowing as the capitalization rate. If the amount of a specific borrowing that is incurred to construct a specific asset is less than the expenditures made for the asset, use a weighted average of the rates applicable to other company borrowings for any excess expenditures over the amount of the project-specific borrowing.

EXAMPLE

Milford Public Sound incurs an average expenditure over the construction period of an outdoor arena complex of $15,000,000. It has taken out a short-term loan of $12,000,000 at 9% interest specifically to cover the cost of this project. Milford can capitalize the interest cost of the entire amount of the $12,000,000 loan at 9% interest, but it still has $3,000,000 of average expenditures that exceed the amount of this project-specific loan.

Milford has two bonds outstanding at the time of the project, in the following amounts:

Bond Description		Principal Outstanding	Interest
8% Bond		$18,000,000	$1,440,000
10% Bond		12,000,000	1,200,000
	Totals	$30,000,000	$2,640,000

The weighted-average interest rate on these two bond issuances is 8.8% ($2,640,000 interest ÷ $30,000,000 principal), which is the interest rate that Milford should use when capitalizing the remaining $3,000,000 of average expenditures.

These rules regarding the formulation of the capitalization rate are subject to some interpretation. The key guideline is to arrive at a *reasonable* measure of the cost of financing the acquisition of a fixed asset, particularly in regard to the interest cost that could have been avoided if the acquisition had not been made. Thus, it is possible to use a selection of outstanding borrowings as the basis for a weighted average calculation. This may result in the inclusion or exclusion of borrowings at the corporate level, or just at the level of the subsidiary where the asset is located.

EXAMPLE

Milford Public Sound (MPS) has issued several bonds and notes, totaling $50,000,000, that are used to fund both general corporate activities and construction projects. It also has access to a low-cost 4% internal line of credit that is extended to it by its corporate parent, Milford Sound. MPS regularly uses this line of credit for short-term activities, and typically draws the balance down to zero at least once a year. The average amount of this line that is outstanding is approximately $10,000,000 at any given time.

Since the corporate line of credit comprises a significant amount of MPS's ongoing borrowings, and there is no restriction that prevents these funds from being used for construction projects, it would be reasonable to include the interest cost of this line of credit in the calculation of the weighted-average cost of borrowings that is used to derive MPS's capitalization rate.

Calculating Interest Capitalization

Follow these steps to calculate the amount of interest to be capitalized for a specific project:

1. Construct a table itemizing the amounts of expenditures made and the dates on which the expenditures were made.
2. Determine the date on which interest capitalization ends.
3. Calculate the capitalization period for each expenditure, which is the number of days between the specific expenditure and the end of the interest capitalization period.
4. Divide each capitalization period by the total number of days elapsed between the date of the first expenditure and the end of the interest capitalization period to arrive at the capitalization multiplier for each line item.
5. Multiply each expenditure amount by its capitalization multiplier to arrive at the average expenditure for each line item over the capitalization measurement period.
6. Add up the average expenditures at the line item level to arrive at a grand total average expenditure.
7. If there is project-specific debt, multiply the grand total of the average expenditures by the interest rate on that debt to arrive at the capitalized interest related to that debt.
8. If the grand total of the average expenditures exceeds the amount of the project-specific debt, multiply the excess expenditure amount by the weighted average of the company's other outstanding debt to arrive at the remaining amount of interest to be capitalized.
9. Add together both capitalized interest calculations. If the combined total is more than the total interest cost incurred by the company during the calculation period, reduce the amount of interest to be capitalized to the total interest cost incurred by the company during the calculation period.
10. Record the interest capitalization with a debit to the project's fixed asset account and a credit to the interest expense account.

EXAMPLE

Milford Public Sound is building a concert arena. Milford makes payments related to the project of $10,000,000 and $14,000,000 to a contractor on January 1 and July 1, respectively. The arena is completed on December 31.

For the 12-month period of construction, Milford can capitalize all of the interest on the $10,000,000 payment, since it was outstanding during the full period of construction. Milford can capitalize the interest on the $14,000,000 payment for half of the construction period, since it was outstanding during only the second half of the construction period. The average expenditure for which the interest cost can be capitalized is calculated in the following table.

Date of Payment	Expenditure Amount	Capitalization Period*	Capitalization Multiplier	Average Expenditure
January 1	$10,000,000	12 months	12/12 months = 100%	$10,000,000
July 1	14,000,000	6 months	6/12 months = 50%	7,000,000
				$17,000,000

* In the table, the capitalization period is defined as the number of months that elapse between the expenditure payment date and the end of the interest capitalization period.

The only debt that Milford has outstanding during this period is a line of credit, on which the interest rate is 8%. The maximum amount of interest that Milford can capitalize into the cost of this arena project is $1,360,000, which is calculated as:

8% Interest rate × $17,000,000 Average expenditure = $1,360,000

Milford records the following journal entry:

	Debit	Credit
Fixed assets – Arena	1,360,000	
Interest expense		1,360,000

Tip: There may be an inordinate number of expenditures related to a larger project, which could result in a large and unwieldy calculation of average expenditures. To reduce the workload, consider aggregating these expenses by month, and then assume that each expenditure was made in the middle of the month, thereby reducing all of the expenditures for each month to a single line item.

It is not allowable to capitalize more interest cost in an accounting period than the total amount of interest cost incurred by the business in that period. If there is a corporate parent, this rule means that the amount capitalized cannot exceed the total amount of interest cost incurred by the business on a consolidated basis.

Summary

The key issue with interest capitalization is whether to use it at all. It requires a certain amount of administrative effort to compile, and so is not recommended for lower-value assets. Instead, reserve its use for larger projects where including the cost of interest in an asset will improve the quality of the financial information reported by the entity. It should *not* be used merely to delay the recognition of interest expense. If the choice is made to use interest capitalization, adopt a procedure for determining the amount to be capitalized and closely adhere to it, with appropriate documentation of the results. This will result in a standardized calculation methodology that auditors can more easily review.

Interest Capitalization

When examining proposed project contracts with customers, be sure to include the cost of interest in the amount to be reimbursed by the customer. This is especially important for longer-term projects that require a substantial up-front investment. If this cost reimbursement is not included, the seller's potential profit could be seriously reduced.

Chapter 6
Additional Project Accounting Topics

Introduction

Besides the cost accumulation and revenue recognition subjects discussed in the preceding chapters, there are several additional topics within GAAP that are closely related to project accounting. When the amount of costs ascribed to a project have exceeded expectations, it may be necessary to charge some portion of the cost to expense in the current period, as described in the following Asset Impairment section. It is also possible that a project may involve research and development activities, internal-use software, or the development of a website. All of these topics are covered in the following sections.

Asset Impairment

There are rules under GAAP for periodically testing assets to see if they are still as valuable as the costs at which they were recorded in the project accounting records. If not, reduce the recorded cost of these assets by recognizing a loss. Also, under no circumstances is it allowable to reverse an impairment loss under GAAP.

An impairment loss should be recognized for a fixed asset if its carrying amount is not recoverable and exceeds its fair value. Recognize this loss within income from continuing operations on the income statement.

The carrying amount of an asset is not recoverable if it exceeds the sum of the undiscounted cash flows that are expected to result from the use of the asset over its remaining useful life and the final disposition of the asset. These cash flow estimates should incorporate assumptions that are reasonable in relation to the assumptions the entity uses for its budgets, forecasts, and so forth. If there are a range of possible cash flow outcomes, consider using a probability-weighted cash flow analysis.

Only test for the recoverability of an asset whenever the circumstances indicate that its carrying amount may not be recoverable. Examples of such situations are:

- *Cash flow.* There are historical and projected operating or cash flow losses associated with the asset.
- *Costs.* There are excessive costs incurred to acquire or construct the asset.
- *Disposal.* The asset is more than 50% likely to be sold or otherwise disposed of significantly before the end of its previously estimated useful life.
- *Legal.* There is a significant adverse change in legal factors or the business climate that could affect the asset's value.
- *Market price.* There is a significant decrease in the asset's market price.
- *Usage.* There is a significant adverse change in the asset's manner of use, or in its physical condition.

If there is an impairment at the level of an asset group, allocate the impairment among the assets in the group on a pro rata basis, based on the carrying amounts of the assets in the group. However, the impairment loss cannot reduce the carrying amount of an asset below its fair value.

Tip: You only have to determine the fair value of an asset for this test if it is "determinable without undue cost and effort." Thus, if an outside appraisal would be required to determine fair value, you can likely dispense with this requirement and simply allocate the impairment loss to all of the assets in the group.

EXAMPLE

Luminescence Corporation is constructing a small floodlight manufacturing facility. Luminescence considers the entire facility to be a group of assets, so it conducts an impairment test on the entire operation. The test reveals that a continuing decline in the market for floodlights (caused by the surge in LED lights in the market) has caused a $2 million impairment charge. Luminescence allocates the charge to the four assets in the facility as follows:

Asset	Carrying Amount	Proportion of Carrying Amounts	Impairment Allocation	Revised Carrying Amount
Ribbon machine	$8,000,000	67%	$1,340,000	$6,660,000
Conveyors	1,500,000	13%	260,000	1,240,000
Gas injector	2,000,000	16%	320,000	1,680,000
Filament inserter	500,000	4%	80,000	420,000
Totals	$12,000,000	100%	$2,000,000	$10,000,000

Research and Development Costs

Research and development involves those activities that create or improve products or processes. Examples of activities typically considered to fall within the research and development functional area are noted in the following table.

Research and Development Activities

Research to discover new knowledge	Modifying formulas, products, or processes
Applying new research findings	Designing and testing prototypes
Formulating product and process designs	Designing tools that involve new technology
Testing products and processes	Designing and operating a pilot plant

The basic problem with research and development expenditures is that the future benefits associated with these expenditures are sufficiently uncertain that it is difficult to record the expenditures as an asset. Given these uncertainties, GAAP mandates that all research and development expenditures be charged to expense as incurred. The chief variance from this guidance is in a business combination, where the acquirer can recognize the fair value of research and development assets.

The basic rule of charging all research and development expenditures to expense is not entirely pervasive, since there are exceptions, as noted below:

- *Assets.* If materials or fixed assets have been acquired that have alternative future uses, record them as assets. The materials should be charged to expense as consumed, while depreciation should be used to gradually reduce the carrying amount of the fixed assets. Conversely, if there are no alternative future uses, charge these costs to expense as incurred.
- *Computer software.* If computer software is acquired for use in a research and development project, charge the cost to expense as incurred. However, if there are future alternative uses for the software, capitalize its cost and depreciate the software over its useful life.
- *Contracted services.* If the company is billed by third parties for research work conducted on behalf of the company, charge these invoices to expense.
- *Indirect costs.* A reasonable amount of overhead expenses should be allocated to research and development activities.
- *Purchased intangibles.* If intangible assets are acquired from third parties and these assets have alternative uses, they are to be accounted for as intangible assets. However, if the intangibles are purchased for a specific research project and there are no alternative future uses, charge them to expense as incurred.
- *Software development.* If software is developed for use in research and development activities, charge the associated costs to expense as incurred, without exception.
- *Wages.* Charge the costs of salaries, wages, and related costs to expense as incurred.

> **Tip:** "Alternative future uses" can include other research and development projects, or other uses.

There may also be research and development arrangements where a third party (a sponsor) provides funding for the research and development activities of a business. The arrangements may be designed to shift licensing rights, intellectual property ownership, an equity stake, or a share in the profits to the sponsors. The business conducting the research and development activities may be paid a fixed fee or some form of cost reimbursement arrangement by the sponsors.

When an entity is a party to a research and development arrangement, several accounting issues must be resolved, which are:

- *Loans or advances issued.* If the business lends or advances funds to third parties, and repayment is based entirely on whether there are economic benefits associated with the research and development work, charge these amounts to expense.

43

- *Nonrefundable advances*. Defer the recognition of any nonrefundable advance payments that will be used for research and development activities, and recognize them as expenses when the related goods are delivered or services performed. If at any point it is not expected that the goods will be delivered or services performed, charge the remaining deferred amount to expense.
- *Obligation to perform services*. If repayment of the funds provided by the funding parties is solely dependent upon the results of the related research and development activities, account for the repayment obligation as a contract to perform work for others.
- *Repayment obligation*. If there is an obligation to repay the funding parties or the business has indicated an intent to do so, no matter what the outcome of the research and development may be, recognize a liability for the amount of the repayment, and charge research and development costs to expense as incurred. This accounting is also required if there is a significant related party relationship between the business and the funding entities. This scenario also applies if the funding parties can require the business to purchase their interest in the partnership, or if the funding parties automatically receive securities from the business upon termination of the arrangement.

Internal-Use Software

Companies routinely develop software for internal use, and want to understand how these development costs are to be accounted for. Software is considered to be for internal use when it has been acquired or developed *only* for the internal needs of a business. Examples of situations where software is considered to be developed for internal use are:

- Accounting systems
- Cash management tracking systems
- Membership tracking systems
- Production automation systems

Further, there can be no reasonably possible plan to market the software outside of the company. A market feasibility study is not considered a reasonably possible marketing plan. However, a history of selling software that had initially been developed for internal use creates a reasonable assumption that the latest internal-use product will also be marketed for sale outside of the company.

The accounting for internal-use software varies, depending upon the stage of completion of the project. The relevant accounting is:

- *Stage 1: Preliminary*. All costs incurred during the preliminary stage of a development project should be charged to expense as incurred. This stage is considered to include making decisions about the allocation of resources, determining performance requirements, conducting supplier demonstrations, evaluating technology, and supplier selection.

- *Stage 2: Application development.* Capitalize the costs incurred to develop internal-use software, which may include coding, hardware installation, and testing. Any costs related to data conversion, user training, administration, and overhead should be charged to expense as incurred. Only the following costs can be capitalized:
  - Materials and services consumed in the development effort, such as third party development fees, software purchase costs, and travel costs related to development work.
  - The payroll costs of those employees directly associated with software development.
  - The capitalization of interest costs incurred to fund the project.

- *Stage 3. Post-implementation.* Charge all post-implementation costs to expense as incurred. Samples of these costs are training and maintenance costs.

Any allowable capitalization of costs should begin *after* the preliminary stage has been completed, management commits to funding the project, it is probable that the project will be completed, and the software will be used for its intended function.

The capitalization of costs should end when all substantial testing has been completed. If it is no longer probable that a project will be completed, stop capitalizing the costs associated with it, and conduct impairment testing on the costs already capitalized (see the preceding Asset Impairment section). The cost at which the asset should then be carried is the lower of its carrying amount or fair value (less costs to sell). Unless there is evidence to the contrary, the usual assumption is that uncompleted software has no fair value.

A business may purchase software for internal use. If the purchase price of this software includes other elements, such as training and maintenance fees, only capitalize that portion of the purchase price that relates to the software itself.

In addition, any later upgrades of the software can be capitalized, but only if it is probable that extra system functionality will result from the upgrade. The costs of maintaining the system should be charged to expense as incurred. If the maintenance is provided by a third party and payment is made in advance for the services of that party, amortize the cost of the maintenance over the service period.

Once costs have been capitalized, amortize them over the expected useful life of the software. This is typically done on a straight-line basis, unless another method more clearly reflects the expected usage pattern of the software. Amortization should begin when a software module is ready for its intended use, which is considered to be when all substantial system testing has been completed. If a software module cannot function unless other modules are also completed, do not begin amortization until the related modules are complete.

It may be necessary to regularly reassess the useful life of the software for amortization purposes, since technological obsolescence tends to shorten it.

Internal-use software should be routinely reviewed for impairment. The following are all indicators of the possible presence of asset impairment:

- The software is not expected to be of substantive use
- The manner in which the software was originally intended to be used has now changed
- The software is to be significantly altered
- The development cost of the software significantly exceeded original expectations

Once a business has developed software for internal use, management may decide to market it for external use by third parties. If so, the proceeds from software licensing, net of selling costs, should be applied against the carrying amount of the software asset. For the purposes of this topic, selling costs are considered to include commissions, software reproduction costs, servicing obligations, warranty costs, and installation costs. The business should not recognize a profit on sales of the software until the application of net sales to the carrying amount of the software asset has reduced the carrying amount to zero. The business can recognize all further proceeds as revenue.

Website Development Costs

A company may allocate funds to the development of a company website, in such areas as coding, graphics design, the addition of content, and site operation. The accounting for website development varies, depending upon the stage of completion of the project. The relevant accounting is:

- *Stage 1: Preliminary.* Charge all site planning costs to expense as incurred. This stage is considered to include project planning, the determination of site functionality, hardware identification, technology usability, alternatives analysis, supplier demonstrations, and legal considerations.
- *Stage 2: Application development and infrastructure.* The accounting matches what was just described in the last section for internal-use software. In essence, capitalize these costs. More specifically, capitalize the cost of obtaining and registering an Internet domain, as well as the procurement of software tools, code customization, web page development, related hardware, hypertext link creation, and site testing. Also, if a site upgrade provides new functions or features to the website, capitalize these costs.
- *Stage 3: Graphics development.* For the purposes of this topic, graphics are considered to be software, and so are capitalized, unless they are to be marketed externally. Graphics development includes site page design and layout.
- *Stage 4: Content development.* Charge data conversion costs to expense as incurred, as well as the costs to input content into a website.

- *Stage 5: Site operation.* The costs to operate a website are the same as any other operating costs, and so should be charged to expense as incurred. The treatment of selected operating costs associated with a website are:
  - Charge website hosting fees to expense over the period benefited by the hosting
  - Charge search engine registration fees to expense as incurred, since they are advertising costs

Summary

Of the topics covered in this chapter, the most broadly applicable one is asset impairment. If a project has a large budget, will span a significant period of time, and there is uncertainty about its outcome, then conduct a series of asset impairment tests over the life of the project. Conversely, if a project covers only a short time period, involves an outcome that has been achieved numerous times before, and calls for only a modest investment, the need for impairment testing is greatly reduced.

Chapter 7
Project Controls

Introduction

The accumulation of costs for a project and subsequent billings to customers can yield unexpected results in a surprising number of ways – either due to fraud, mismanagement or minimal formal processes. The financial and reputational impact of incorrect project costing and billing can be substantial. To mitigate these impacts, we describe in this chapter a number of project controls aggregated by certain contract types, as well as for internal projects.

Controls for Cost Plus Pricing Arrangements

Project controls are especially necessary when a company is billing to a customer under a cost plus pricing arrangement. In this situation, there is a strong temptation to add unauthorized costs to a project in order to bill these costs through to the customer, along with a profit percentage. The following controls can be used to mitigate this risk:

- *Establish cost definitions.* Work with the customer to develop a definition of each type of cost that is to be allowed within a project. This should include the contents of all overhead cost pools. A cost pool is a grouping of individual overhead costs, which are then allocated. Having cost definitions makes it easier to determine whether a cost should be included in or excluded from a project.

> **Tip:** Continue to refine cost definitions over time, as various costs are encountered for which the existing definitions are not sufficiently clear. By doing so, it will become easier to include costs in or exclude them from projects, which in turn leads to fewer conflicts with customers.

- *Establish allocation methodologies.* There may be a temptation to increase the allocation of overhead to a specific project, so that the allocated cost can be billed to a customer. However, doing so will likely result in an irate customer. Consequently, document at the start of a project the allocation calculations that will be used. The internal audit staff can then verify that the established allocation is being used throughout a project.
- *Establish expense approval process.* Have a member of management above the level of the project manager approve the larger expenses before they are incurred. Doing so reduces the risk of incurring inappropriate expenses.

- *Review appropriateness of expenses*. It is possible that excessive or improper costs will be charged to a project. These can be difficult to detect, especially when the amounts charged are relatively small. Nonetheless, there should be a routine internal audit examination of project costs that delves into the applicability of charged expenses. When non-compliant expenses are found in a project, the audit team should not only document these issues, but also trace them back to the person who authorized the original recordation. This may lead to further investigations into other costs authorized by the individual, to see if there is a pattern of over-charging projects.

Controls for Fixed Fee Pricing Arrangements

When a company engages in fixed fee pricing arrangements, there is a certain amount of pressure for project managers to report a profit by the end of a contract. If so, a manager might be tempted to offload expenses elsewhere, rather than charging them to a project that is in danger of having a minimal profit or even a loss. The following controls can be used to mitigate this risk:

- *Use cost checklist*. When first devising a bid for a fixed fee pricing arrangement, use a standard checklist of costs that should be included in the formulation of the bid. It is entirely too easy to forget a major cost, which in turn is difficult for a reviewer to spot, since it is absent from the bidding documentation. Thus, a cost checklist that is based on costs incurred in previous projects is an excellent way to reduce the risk of underbidding.
- *Review percentage of completion*. When a fixed fee arrangement spans a number of months, the seller may be able to recognize some portion of the total revenue prior to final project completion, as outlined in the Project Pricing, Billing and Revenue chapter. The estimation of the amount of revenue to recognize is subject to fraud, since the information used for this determination can be altered, and is subject to interpretation. To mitigate this risk, periodically have a third party review the calculation of the percentage of completion. Better yet, develop a documented methodology for calculating the percentage of completion, and review the ability of managers to follow this process.
- *Conduct milestone reviews*. It is entirely possible under a fixed fee arrangement that the seller will incur more costs than it can recover from the pricing structure of the underlying contract. If so, the amount of costs already incurred that will not be recovered must be charged to expense at once. To aid in making this decision promptly, build into the project timeline a series of milestone reviews. These reviews should examine the costs incurred to date and the projected costs required to complete the project, and make a determination of whether any costs should be written off.
- *Monitor scope changes*. One of the chief causes of losses in a fixed fee arrangement is when the customer demands changes in the scope of the project, and the project manager does not respond with a change order to raise the

price. Instead, the cost of the project spirals upward with no attendant increase in billings to the customer. The best control over scope changes is proper training of the project manager in regard to the nature of scope changes and how to press for a change order. An additional control is to conduct periodic audits of open projects to see if scope creep has occurred without an attendant approval by the customer of a change order.

- *Close completed projects promptly.* Once a project has been completed, close it at once, so that no additional transactions can be charged to it. Otherwise, a canny project manager could charge a cost to it that should belong elsewhere. The charge may not be noticed, since all reporting related to the closed project has already been completed.
- *Conduct closing review.* Once a project has been completed, conduct a formal written review of the project that states the revenues billed and expenses incurred. The project manager should sign off on this document, which is then securely archived. The reason for this review is to establish a record of the amount of approved costs incurred. If the project accounting records later reveal a different cost total, this indicates that the records were subsequently manipulated.
- *Monitor change log.* If project costs are being recorded in a formal accounting database, the accounting system may contain a change log. This is a listing of the user identification numbers of anyone altering the accounting information, including the records changed and the nature of the changes. Turn on this change log, and include in the department's schedule of activities a monthly reminder to examine the log for unusual changes. This task could identify the unapproved shifting of costs between projects.

Controls for Internal Projects

When an organization is engaged in a construction project for its own internal use, there may be a temptation to park costs in an amorphous construction-in-progress account, rather than charging them to expense in the current period. Doing so defers expense recognition. In addition, there is a tendency for internal projects to have cost overruns, usually because the expectations for these projects were poorly defined. The following controls deal with these and other concerns:

- *Assign a project sponsor.* If there is a person in management who is directly responsible for a project, that individual will be quite likely to spend time overseeing its progress. If there is no such individual, a project is much more likely to drag on and accumulate costs.
- *Create a project budget.* There should be a carefully-defined budget for each project. In addition, the project accountant should periodically compare actual costs incurred to this budget, and report material variances to senior management.
- *Lock the project budget.* When a project manager is judged based on a comparison of actual to budgeted results, there is a temptation to increase the size

of the budget. Doing so shrinks any negative variances due to cost overruns. This can be avoided by password-protecting access to the original budget file.

- *Enact a monitoring plan.* There should be a formal system in place that requires managers to examine the progress to date on a project, as well as the costs incurred. Progress can be measured in a number of ways, including:
    - o Hours worked to date
    - o Costs incurred to date
    - o Remaining hours required to complete the project
    - o Remaining costs to be incurred to complete the project
    - o Milestone tasks completed

    Someone with the power to shut down a project should participate in this examination. Otherwise, there is a tendency for the existing project staff to perpetuate a project, since it gives them ongoing employment. It can also be useful to issue status reports in between these formal meetings; adverse information in a status report could trigger an additional review meeting to see if corrective action should be taken.

- *Document project decisions.* If decisions are made during a project to cut back on or increase funding, document the reasons why these decisions were made. This documentation should include an approval signature from the assigned project sponsor or project manager. This control assigns responsibility for actions taken.

- *Conduct impairment reviews.* If there is a risk that the outcome of a construction project will be a failure, conduct regular reviews of the status of the project. If it appears that the project will fail, or that there will be major cost overruns, create an impairment charge in the current period. The amount of this charge could correspond to the entire amount invested in the project to date, if there is no expectation that a usable asset will be created. The amount of the impairment could also be a lesser amount, perhaps reflecting the amount of any cost overruns. See the Additional Project Accounting Topics chapter for more information.

- *Define the expected outcome.* Define the characteristics of what is considered to be a successful outcome of the project. By being as specific as possible, one can then define when such an outcome has been reached, so that a project can be terminated. Otherwise, there is a tendency for it to drag on, accumulating costs.

- *Conduct a post-project review.* Once a project has been completed, compare the original time and cost estimates to the amounts actually incurred. Despite being after-the-fact, this can be considered a control, since a poor project review could impede the career of the sponsoring manager, whose poor estimating abilities or management skills led to an inadequate outcome. Thus, knowing that a post-project review will be conducted could lead a manager to be especially careful in estimating for and managing a project.

Summary

The level of control over project costs related to customer billings should be quite high. The reason is that an overbilling found by a customer's audit team may trigger a penalty clause that requires the company to not only pay back the amount of the overbilling, but also pay an additional penalty. In addition, egregious overbillings may lead to a company being removed from the approved supplier lists of its customers.

Another way of looking at project controls from a customer's perspective is when the seller's internal audit staff decides that a customer was overbilled, and voluntarily issues a payment back to the customer in the amount of the overbilling. This is such an unexpected outcome from the perspective of the customer that the seller may become a preferred supplier to that customer for future projects.

Chapter 8
Project Measurements

Introduction

From the perspective of project accounting, there are only a small number of measurements that are used to evaluate the financial health of a project. An ongoing cost analysis is needed to see if a project in progress is meeting expectations for expenditures, while a free cash flow analysis looks at the net inflow or outflow of cash associated with a project. In addition, three measurements are available for comparing the investment in a project to its earnings or cash flows. The net present value and break-even measurements are used to evaluate whether a project in progress should be continued, while the return on assets is more commonly used to evaluate the results of a project once it has been completed. These measurements are discussed in the following sections.

> **Related Podcast Episodes:** Episodes 70 and 147 of the Accounting Best Practices Podcast discuss breakeven analysis and net present value analysis. They are available at: **accountingtools.com/podcasts** or **iTunes**

Cost Variance

From the perspective of the project accountant, the key project measurement is the amount of cost incurred versus the amount of cost planned. The variance is calculated as follows:

$$\text{Budgeted cost of work} - \text{Actual cost of work} = \text{Cost variance}$$

The variance can also be stated as a ratio of budgeted to actual cost, which is called the cost performance index. The ratio calculation is:

$$\frac{\text{Budgeted cost of work}}{\text{Actual cost of work}}$$

The cost variance can be derived as a look-back measurement, where the actual cost to-date is compared to the budgeted cost to-date. However, this approach does not predict the impact of future changes in costs, and so gives management no insights into what cost variances are likely to arise before a project has been completed. This additional level of reporting requires a constant analysis of the percentage of completion of each task, and conversations with project team members to formulate projections of the costs that must still be incurred. Thus, a forward-looking cost variance is a constantly changing number, and so must be continually revised to reflect the latest progress toward the goal of a project. Given the continually changing cost estimates, it can make sense to report the cost variance for the entire duration of a project, including the cumulative variance to date. The following exhibit illustrates the concept.

Sample Cost Variance Report

Month	Budgeted Cost	Actual Cost	Variance	Cumulative Variance
January	$100,000	$105,000	-$5,000	-$5,000
February	80,000	82,000	-2,000	-7,000
March	75,000	93,000	-18,000	-25,000
April	110,000	104,000	+6,000	-19,000
May	50,000	62,000	-12,000	-31,000

Net Present Value

Net present value (NPV) involves the determination of expected cash flows from a project over its lifespan, and discounting these cash flows back to their present value. This technique is commonly used when deciding whether to provide initial funding for a project. However, it can also be used on an ongoing basis during a project, as better information about cash flows becomes available. This constant review of a project's NPV is highly recommended, since it can reveal that the initial assumptions about a project's cash flows were so incorrect that the project should be curtailed prior to completion.

To derive a net present value analysis, enter the most recent estimate of cash flows for a project in a spreadsheet, and then apply a discount rate that reduces the cash flows to what they would be worth at the present date. A discount rate is the interest rate used to discount a stream of future cash flows to their present value, typically using an organization's cost of capital.

EXAMPLE

Milagro Corporation's project accountant is reviewing the latest update to the cash flows expected from a project for the next five years. Milagro's cost of capital is 10%, which is used as the discount rate to construct the net present value of the project. The following table shows the calculation:

Year	Cash Flow	10% Discount Factor	Present Value
0	-$500,000	1.0000	-$500,000
1	+130,000	0.9091	+118,183
2	+130,000	0.8265	+107,445
3	+130,000	0.7513	+97,669
4	+130,000	0.6830	−88,790
5	+130,000	0.6209	+80,717
		Net Present Value	−$7,196

The net present value of the proposed project is negative at the 10% discount rate, so the project accountant calls a meeting with the project manager and project sponsor to decide whether adjustments should be made to the project.

In the "10% Discount Factor" column, the factor becomes smaller for periods further in the future, because the discounted value of cash flows are reduced as they progress further from the present day.

A net present value calculation that truly reflects the reality of cash flows will likely be more complex than the one shown in the preceding example. It is best to break down the analysis into a number of sub-categories, to see exactly when cash flows are occurring and with what activities they are associated. Here are the more common contents of a net present value analysis:

- *Asset purchases*. All of the expenditures associated with the purchase, delivery, installation, and testing of the asset being purchased.
- *Asset-linked expenses*. Any ongoing expenses, such as warranty agreements, property taxes, and maintenance, that are associated with the asset.
- *Contribution margin*. Any incremental cash flows resulting from sales that can be attributed to the project.
- *Depreciation effect*. The asset will be depreciated, and this depreciation shelters a portion of any net income from income taxes, so note the income tax reduction caused by depreciation.
- *Expense reductions*. Any incremental expense reductions caused by the project, such as automation that eliminates direct labor hours.
- *Tax credits*. If an asset purchase triggers a tax credit (such as for a purchase of energy-reduction equipment), then note the amount of the credit.
- *Taxes*. Any income tax payments associated with net income expected to be derived from the asset.
- *Working capital changes*. Any net changes in inventory, accounts receivable, or accounts payable associated with the asset. Also, when the asset is eventually sold off, this may trigger a reversal of the initial working capital changes.

By itemizing the preceding factors in a net present value analysis, it is easier to review and revise individual line items.

Net present value is the traditional approach to evaluating project expenditures, since it is based on a single factor – cash flows – that can be used to judge any expenditure proposal arriving from anywhere in a company. However, the net present value method can be a poor evaluation method if there is a suspicion that the cash flows used to derive an analysis are incorrect. If so, consider using scenario analysis and sensitivity analysis to make a closer examination of the situation.

Scenario analysis involves modeling of specific situations that can impact cash flows, such as the impact of an airliner crash on the willingness of the public to use air transport. Sensitivity analysis involves modeling changes in the key assumptions underlying an NPV analysis, such as market share or the costs of labor, utilities, and rent. These additional analyses are intended to note the extent to which cash flows may change. Here are several examples of the analyses that could be used for different types of capital expenditures:

- *Production equipment*. If equipment is being purchased to expand production capacity, use sensitivity analysis to examine the incremental increases in sales volume that are likely to be expected, with particular attention to the minimum amount of additional sales growth that must occur in order to generate enough cash flow to pay for the machinery.
- *Retail store*. Use sensitivity analysis to model seasonal sales levels to determine cash flows at different times of the year. Also use scenario analysis to model for the impact of a direct competitor opening a store within a short distance of the proposed location.
- *Distribution facility*. Use sensitivity analysis to model the impact of changes in labor costs on the operation of the proposed facility, as well as changes in the cost of fuel to move inventory into and out of the proposed location.
- *Transportation service*. Examples of transportation services are ferries, cruise lines, airlines, and tour buses. Use scenario analysis to model the impact on cash flows of major accidents within the industry, increases in fuel costs due to Middle East conflicts, and changes in public concerns about disease transmission in public spaces.

Scenario analysis and sensitivity analysis can be re-visited throughout a project, to see if the underlying assumptions have changed.

EXAMPLE

Explorer Cruise Lines is contemplating the construction of a cruise ship that will circumnavigate Africa on an ongoing basis. The intent is to dock at major ports frequently, and send passengers inland on multi-day safaris. The initial analysis of potential cash flows indicates that this venture could be extremely profitable. However, a scenario analysis addresses the public's perception of pirates off the east coast of Africa, and the presence of the Ebola virus along the west coast, as well as political unrest along the north coast. All of these scenarios point toward the potential for massive declines in the number of paying passengers. Consequently, Explorer elects to restrict the proposed travel route to the South African and Namibian coastal regions, which are perceived to be safer.

Breakeven Analysis

The breakeven point is the sales volume at which a project earns exactly no money. The concept can be used in the ongoing analysis of projects to determine the minimum sales level at which an investment will earn a profit of zero. This information can be used to develop the minimum baseline of activity that a proposed project must achieve. Management can then use its best judgment to decide whether this minimum activity level can be met. This analysis is commonly made at the start of a project, but should also be made over the course of the project, as better information is obtained about costs and the margins that will likely be obtained in the market. This analysis can result in an ongoing go or no go decision, where management has the option of continuing with a project or killing it.

To calculate the breakeven point, divide total fixed expenses by the contribution margin. Contribution margin is sales minus all variable expenses, divided by sales. The formula is:

$$\frac{\text{Total fixed expenses}}{\text{Contribution margin percentage}}$$

EXAMPLE

Sheep Chops is a meat processing company that is contemplating the construction of a new meat packing facility for sheep, to be located in Wyoming. The facility is expected to incur $6,000,000 of annual labor and other costs. Labor costs only vary slightly with volume, since approximately the same number of employees are needed to staff the production line. In essence, this means that the entire operational cost of the facility is fixed. The current market price for an unprocessed lamb is $0.80 per pound, and the wholesale price for processed lamb is $2.00. This means that the contribution margin of the facility will be 60%, which is calculated as follows:

($2.00 Processed price - $0.80 Unprocessed price) ÷ $2.00 Processed price = 60%

Based on the contribution margin, the breakeven sales level is $10,000,000, which is calculated as follows:

$$\frac{\$6,000,000 \text{ Total fixed expenses}}{60\% \text{ Contribution margin percentage}}$$

= $10,000,000 Breakeven sales level

The current "most likely" scenario indicates that the facility can generate $12,000,000 of sales at current price points, which equates to profitability of $1,200,000, which is calculated as follows:

($12,000,000 Sales × 60% Contribution margin) - $6,000,000 Fixed costs
= $1,200,000 Profit

A further analysis of the situation indicates that a large proportion of the world's sheep products are being diverted to China to meet an increased demand for lamb chops in that country. This increases the scarcity of lamb products in the United States, which will likely keep prices high. Management elects to enter into long-term supply contracts with several ranchers, thereby locking in an assured supply for the next ten years. The assumption of high prices and the action taken to assure supplies places the company in a position to reap excellent cash flows from the new facility for a number of years.

Return on Assets

A certain amount of asset investment is likely to be needed for any project. This may be in the form of fixed assets or working capital, or perhaps the purchase of an intangible asset (such as a patent) from a third party. Whatever the investment may be, a reasonable question to ask is the return being generated on this investment.

The generic return on assets measurement is designed to measure the total return from all sources of income from all assets associated with a project. The formula is:

$$\frac{\text{Net income}}{\text{Total assets}}$$

The measurement is certainly a simple one, but its all-encompassing nature also means that the result may not yield the type of information needed. Consider the following issues:

- *Non-operating income*. The numerator of the ratio is net income, which includes income from all sources, some of which may not be even remotely related to the assets of the business. For example, net income may include interest income from funds invested in a project, but for which there is no immediate use. This issue can be avoided by only using operating income in the numerator.
- *Tax rate*. The net income figure is net of the company's income tax liability. This liability is a result of the company's tax strategy, which may yield an inordinately low (or high) tax rate. Also, depending on the tax strategy, the tax rate could change markedly from year to year. Because of the effect of tax planning, a non-operational technical issue could have a major impact on the calculated amount of return on assets for a project. This concern can be sidestepped by only using before-tax information in the measurement.
- *Cash basis*. The net income figure can be significantly skewed if a project is accounted for using the cash basis of accounting, where transactions are recorded when cash is received or paid out. This issue can be avoided by only using the accrual basis of accounting for a project.

Given these problems, we suggest an alternative measurement, which uses operating income in the numerator. The formula is:

$$\frac{\text{Operating income}}{\text{Total assets}}$$

EXAMPLE

Aquifers International has just won a contract to drill a 10-mile tunnel to transport water from a reservoir to a major city. The company constructs a customized $8,000,000 tunnel boring machine for this project. In the first year of the project, the customer pays the project $6,000,000 and Aquifers incurs $4,800,000 of operating expenses, resulting in operating income of $1,200,000. The resulting calculation of the project's return on investment is:

$$\frac{\$1,200,000 \text{ Operating income}}{\$8,000,000 \text{ Assets}}$$

$$= 15\% \text{ Return on assets}$$

Free Cash Flow

Free cash flow is the net change in cash generated by a project during a reporting period, minus cash outlays for working capital and capital expenditures during the same period. Thus, the calculation of free cash flow is:

Operating cash flow ± Working capital changes − Capital Expenditures

The "operating cash flow" component of that equation is calculated as:

Net income + Depreciation + Amortization

Free cash flow is important because it is an indicator of the financial health of a project. However, there can be a variety of situations in which a project can report positive free cash flow, and which are due to circumstances not necessarily related to a healthy long-term situation. For example, positive free cash flow can be caused by:

- Selling off major assets
- Cutting back on or delaying capital expenditures
- Delaying the payment of accounts payable
- Accelerating receivable receipts with high-cost early payment discounts
- Cutting back on key maintenance expenditures
- Reducing marketing expenditures
- Curtailing scheduled pay increases

In these examples, management has taken steps to reduce the long-term viability of a project in order to improve its short-term free cash flows.

Free cash flow can also be impacted by the growth rate of a project. If a project is growing rapidly, it requires a significant investment in accounts receivable and inventory, which increases its working capital investment and therefore decreases the amount of free cash flow. Conversely, if a project is shrinking, it is converting some of its working capital back into cash as receivables are paid off and inventory liquidated, resulting in an increasing amount of free cash flow.

Summary

There is a strong emphasis in this chapter on the kill decision – whether the funding for a project should be cancelled, based on an ongoing analysis of progress and the amount of funds invested to date. This orientation is especially necessary in large-investment projects where there is considerable uncertainty regarding the outcome of the project. In these situations, a company must guard its available cash by being willing to shut down projects that do not appear to be fulfilling their early promise. This orientation is less necessary in situations where projects are of short duration, require reduced investments, and have relatively certain outcomes.

Glossary

A

Allowance. A lump-sum estimate used in place of a more precise estimate.

C

Capitalization rate. The interest rate used to calculate the amount of interest cost that is recognized as an asset, as part of an asset construction project.

Change order. A formal agreement to modify a contract to change the requirements, duration, or price of a project.

Completed contract method. A method used to recognize the revenue associated with a project as of the end of a project.

Contingency. A buffer of additional funds added to a budget, which is used to compensate for possible inaccuracies and uncertainties.

Cost of capital. The weighted average cost of a company's debt, preferred stock, and common stock.

Cost pool. A grouping of overhead costs that will be allocated.

Cost plus pricing. A contract allowing the seller to bill all costs incurred on a project to the customer, along with a designated profit percentage.

D

Direct cost. A cost that would not exist if a project or other activity did not exist.

Discount rate. The interest rate used to discount a stream of future cash flows to their present value.

F

Fixed fee pricing. A contract requiring the seller to accept a fixed payment amount from the customer.

I

Impairment. The decline in value of an asset below its recorded cost.

Interest capitalization. The recordation of interest costs as an asset when the interest is related to the completion of an asset.

M

Milestone. A scheduled event that represents the completion of a deliverable.

O

Overhead cost. Those costs needed to run a business, but for which there is no clear cause-and-effect relationship with a business activity, product, or service.

P

Percentage of completion method. A method used to derive the amount of revenue associated with a project that can be recognized, based on some measure of the stage of completion.

Index

www.ingramcontent.com/pod-product-compliance
Lightning Source LLC
Chambersburg PA
CBHW051421200326
41520CB00023B/7323